CW00957757

ZODIAC

WOLVERHAMPTON

Edited by Simon Harwin

First published in Great Britain in 2002 by
YOUNG WRITERS
Remus House,
Coltsfoot Drive,
Peterborough, PE2 9JX
Telephone (01733) 890066

HB ISBN 0 75433 606 9
SB ISBN 0 75433 607 7

FOREWORD

Young Writers was established in 1991 with the aim of promoting creative writing in children, to make reading and writing poetry fun.

Once again, this year proved to be a tremendous success with over 41,000 entries received nationwide.

The Zodiac competition has shown us the high standard of work and effort that children are capable of today. The competition has given us a vivid insight into the thoughts and experiences of today's younger generation. It is a reflection of the enthusiasm and creativity that teachers have injected into their pupils, and it shines clearly within this anthology.

The task of selecting poems was a difficult one, but nevertheless, an enjoyable experience. We hope you are as pleased with the final selection in *Zodiac Wolverhampton* as we are.

CONTENTS

The Poems

2020

Get into the time machine,
Forward we go
To 2020,
The world we don't know.
There could be robots
That eat Milky Bars,
I could have a holiday
On planet Mars.
The weather is controlled
By a weather machine,
You can change it to
Whatever you dream.
Cars can fly and swim too,
Look out for shopping trollies
Saying 'Choo, choo.'
Don't be surprised
When it comes to this year,
But now I must go,
My time machine is here.

Kirsty Cartwright (13)
Aldersley High School

TOM OF WOLF CREEK

As little Tom of Wolf Creek slipped off to sleep,
He was woken by an almighty shriek.
He sat up in bed and listened to the cry,
Then it stopped, he let out a sigh.

The next night came and so did the cry,
He asked himself some questions, who, what, where, why?
But had no answers for the questions in his head,
So he snuggled up in his nice warm bed.

The next night he heard a knock on the door,
'I need to come in,' said a voice. Tom replied, 'What for?'
Then he saw a hand of a hairy sort,
That can't be my mom or dad, he thought.

Then the door opened with a slight creak,
He heard again the shuddering shriek.
He opened the curtains and this is what he saw,
A human face with a werewolf claw.

He backed away and turned to see
The werewolves were his family.
He tried to resist, but he lost the fight,
What came next was a werewolf *bite!*

Richard Long (13)
Heath Park High School

THE CURSE OF THE BARN

There was a traveller who came from nowhere,
Who came from far away on a donkey.
He was a funny kind of mysterious person,
With a funny, mysterious face.

This mysterious traveller had to bring a message
To this creepy-looking village.
As he passed the pushy trees,
He felt a cool breeze and he froze.
His beady, ice-blue eyes stared through
The black, moonless night.

He got to a barn door, he heard a spooky, screaming noise.
He turned round, nobody was screaming behind him,
He pushed the barn door open, he saw a little baby lamb,
Lying in the hay, crying out for help as it was about to be slaughtered.

Santana McAill (12)
Heath Park High School

MOVING ON

Each day I sit and watch the sky,
Thinking that your plane would pass on by,
But oh I knew I was so wrong,
As all the planes had come and gone.
But even though I sit alone,
Abandoned by my childhood fantasy,
I know that somewhere far out there,
You would find it in your heart to love.

To love each day as you loved me
And open up your eyes to see
That things that're gone, no longer last
And all of which was in the past.
But as I sit here in your chair,
I know exactly what you fear,
To be alone or to be free,
Although there are things I could not see,
But either way, it's for the best
That things will finally be at rest,
And though I try so hard to lie,
These feelings will not fade or die.
There's only one thing I can do,
Which is to keep away from you,
That when I am feeling sad or blue,
I will not have to turn to you.
So that's the way it's got to go,
It's for the best and we both know.

Alecia Hall (15)
Heath Park High School

BROKEN HEART

He said he cared for me,
That I was the one,
The only woman he had ever loved
And the only one he ever would.

He broke my heart
And he stole my trust,
One thing that can never
Be replaced, is love.

He said he felt for me,
That our love would last for eternity,
That I was the sunlight in his life,
But now he's the darkness over my happiness.

He broke my heart
And he stole my trust,
One thing that can never
Be replaced, is love.

He said we were a match made in heaven,
That I was his queen and he was my king.
Whatever went wrong I will never know,
'Cause now he's gone and left me all alone.

He broke my heart
And he stole my trust,
One thing that can never
Be replaced, is love.

Emma Wright (15)
Heath Park High School

My Bedroom - Enter At Your Own Risk

My bedroom is as small as a box,
It's also as messy as a bombsite.
My bed's never made,
Magazines all over the place
And the stereo's constantly on,
Blasting out music like you're at a concert.
At night, it becomes my haven
Where I sit and watch telly for hours on end.
I love my bedroom,
It's my own special place!

Jennifer Godson (15)
Heath Park High School

A LOVE SO STRONG!

Our love was like an eternal flame,
Our hearts were joined together.
We would never be apart,
We were meant to last forever.

When times were bad and we fell out,
It was never for very long,
Because our love was meant to be
And had grown to be so strong.

We shared our happiest moments,
We shared our secrets too,
No matter what some people said,
No one compared with you.

You had made my life complete
And showed me the meaning of true love,
I didn't know how to thank you,
You were like an angel from above.

It broke my heart to lose you,
The love we had was so strong,
I wish I could turn back the clock
And make our love last forever long.

Rachael Cartwright (15)
Heath Park High School

ROBERT

When I was nine years old,
My mom fostered a four-year-old,
Battered and bruised by parents and life.
They said he was disturbed,
And he certainly disturbed me,
Throwing books, banging guns,
Bringing an end to peace.

Five years later, he moved on
To more permanent carers,
An Asian family in sunny Moseley.
I could not bear to see him go
And went out with friends
At the hour of departure.
No more banging, no more throwing.
Peace has returned,
But the silence is uneasy
And I am uneasy.
Robert, I hope the sun is shining on you.

Mark Chambers (14)
Heath Park High School

THE CURSE

I'm cursed, I'm cursed,
I'm always so naughty.

I'm like a tomboy,
I climb on tress
And get in trouble.

I jump off boxes,
I'm mad and crazy.

I play tricks
With my family.

I can hear my mom
Shouting at me now.

Why does it have to be me?
Why am I so naughty?

I'm sorry mom and everyone,
Just get me out of this curse.

Amanda Gibbs (12)
Heath Park High School

NIGHT NOISES

The door's moving,
Thieves grooving,
The wind blowing,
Weird neighbours mowing.

Radiators clicking,
Leaves flicking,
Cats blinking,
Ghostly smells stinking.

Stars shooting,
Owls hooting,
Fireworks banging,
Thieves ganging.

Clocks tick-tocking,
The rocking horse rocking,
Taps leaking,
Ghosts weeping.

You're sure to get a big fright
From things that go bump in the night.

Daljit Thandi (13)
Heath Park High School

THE CURSE OF THE HEATH PARK MURDERER

As the murderer goes slowly by,
As a little quiet fly,
The murderer knocks on the door, thump, thump, thump.
The boy's heart goes bump, bump, bump.
No one has seen him before,
But he strikes by knocking on a door.
Every day he makes a cunning plan,
His next victim will be a boy or a man.
The people make a plan of their own,
It will be heard because he is as strong as bone.
They will kill him as he comes through the door,
They will grab him, kill him on the floor.

Jagdeep Sangha (13)
Heath Park High School

THE GHOST

In the dark house
Was a squeaky mouse.
A window cracked,
I lay on my back,
A ghost came up and said, 'Boo!'

I heard the church bell,
I heard the victim tell,
A witch came down
And came to town,
A ghost came up and said, 'Boo!'

I saw that ghost,
It went through the post.
I came up and said, 'Boo!'

Vicki Green (12)
Heath Park High School

THE CURSE

An evil cry echoed
Through the ruins of a ghostly hall,
The clanging of a shackle,
No one around, no one at all!

Except a whitish image
Which sent a shiver down your spine.
Another clanging of a shackle,
And a nasty, rusty cackle!

All of a sudden
From out of the gloom,
A bright flash flashed,
Another evil cackle,
The curse has been done!

Emma Jones (13)
Heath Park High School

NIGHT NOISES

Pete was lying in his bed
Trying to get to sleep.
He heard creaking noises,
He got scared,
He could tell it wasn't his dad or mom.
The thing walked into his room,
It walked towards him,
He covered himself up.
It got closer and closer,
It was really dark.
His mom and dad were in bed.
Pete tried to call his parents,
But they didn't hear him.
Then the thing jumped onto his bed,
It was only his cat,
His very own black cat called Tom.

Jason Lavender (12)
Heath Park High School

The Evil Curse

T   errifying screams,
H   ate-filled spirits,
E   vil devils.

E   vil curses,
V   ampires that suck blood,
I   nvisible traps,
L   ooming monsters.

C   andles,
U   ncanny things,
R   ustling sounds,
S   hadowy things,
E   erie movements.

Matthew Whittaker (13)
Heath Park High School

THE CURSE

This is the curse of your bed,
Deadly at night,
All sleeping tight,
Snug up in bed,
With all sleepy heads.
Soon to be dawn,
When they get a thorn,
Just a bit of a surprise
When they go to rise.
Now this is the curse of your bed.

Georgina Potter (12)
Heath Park High School

THE SWIFT

The swift flies without a sound,
Riding thermals round and round,
School kids run around the grounds,
Below the wood's church spire.

Spiritual figures lurk,
As people in houses work,
Where the swift flies up above,
Joining up with flocks of doves.

Army commanders scream and shout
As the swift dodges in and out,
Shrapnel deadly, shooting up,
Moonlit mountains shimmer.

Gavin Gill (13)
Heath Park High School

DOWN IN THE BASEMENT

Down in the basement there is no light,
All that gleams is a nasty sight.
There it sits and there it stares,
A nasty thing, dare, it glares,
Down in the basement of Heath Park.

When it eats, it eats like a monster,
When it roars, it roars like a lion,
When it gets out, run and shout,
Lock the doors, don't let it out,
Down in the basement of Heath Park.

So beware when you go down,
You'll find it's there,
In the basement of Heath Park.

Toni Moreton (13)
Heath Park High School

THE CURSE OF SPRINGDALE

As the wind blew, the night had set with a full moon
To light up the village of Springdale.
All the villagers were terrorised by the wicked villain of Springdale.
No one had enough courage to go up to the villain and stand up
for themselves.
They were treated like dirt.
Everyone thought of a plan, but backed off.
One man had courage and took pride in himself,
So he went to the villain and saw a lamp lit up.
He slyly got the lamp and broke it,
The curse had gone.
The powers of the villain had gone.
Through the pages of history, the hero was lost.

Sandeep Malhi (12)
Heath Park High School

THE CURSE OF THE TOMB!

I was digging in Egypt, I thought
I'd finally got it in my hands,
Then all of a sudden, the winds blew.
I couldn't believe it, all the years I had dug there,
I finally got it, it was the curse of the tomb.

I went into the tomb,
I knew there would be booby traps,
I didn't worry about them.
I felt something grab my shoulder,
It was the curse of the tomb.

I looked around, it was the mummy,
It chased me into this room.
It was filled with treasure, I smiled,
It wasn't the curse of the tomb.

I tried to get out of the room,
I saw skeletons by the treasure,
I thought I was going to die,
It was the curse of the tomb.

Then I saw a trapdoor lever,
I pushed it without a thought,
It opened and all the treasure slid out,
It took me with it.
It was the curse of the tomb.

I was sliding down and down and down,
I couldn't stop myself,
It was like a water slide.
It was the curse of the tomb.

Then I fell into water,
I slid all the way to Africa.
I saw a ship, I was saved.
I've escaped the curse of the tomb.

Kayleigh Beaufoy (12)
Heath Park High School

THE CURSE OF DRAYTON MANOR

Up the hall we walked alone,
Through the moonless night,
Painted walls of monsters down below
Gave me such a fright.

I walked through the passage door,
Brave as a knight,
Shaking floor and flickering lights,
I couldn't see at all.

Knocking, knocking on the door,
No one harkening to my call,
Hearts as cold as ice and walls.

Sitting on a bench, shaking like a leaf,
Suddenly the room was turning
And turning, turning,
All day long.

Dream, dream, dreams can come true.

Elle Chambers (12)
Heath Park High School

ENDLESS

As he walked through the gates and up to the door,
He heard a howling cry,
So he ran into the house but didn't realise what was inside.
He pushed open the door and it creaked out loud,
It slammed behind him and he jumped with fright.
As he walked through the house, the floorboards creaked
And cold chills went down his back.
The corridor was dark, damp and dim
And the wind blew from under the doors.
As he touched the dusty handle and pushed it down,
The hinges squeaked and screamed out with pain.
His heart was pounding and his blood went cold
As he pushed the door open.
He stepped in carefully and peered
And heard a groaning howl.
It was a phantom and they saw each other
Looking into each other's eyes.
The phantom thought, 'That mangy runt will need a shocking death.'
The phantom made an evil presence on the man's soul.
He lifted up and drifted to his future.
Death!

Marc Everitt (13)
Heath Park High School

THE CURSE OF MISS C

It was the last lesson of the day with Miss C,
Then the school bell rang for three o'clock.
A noise came from the loudspeaker,
It was Spooky Sally.

The voice said, 'I will kill you, Miss C,
And burn your bones to ashes.
That's what you've done to me.
Miss killed me!'

Miss C shouted, 'Go away you zombie!
You've risen from the dead, you're scaring my class.
Every day your creaky voice echoes around the room.'
'Miss C, Miss C, I will kill you.'

'Sir, Sir, look in Miss C's window, she's lying on the floor.
I think she's dead as she isn't answering her door.
Her dog is barking,
That is all.'

'Class, I've got some bad news about Miss C.
She was lying on the floor in her dog's space.
She is dead children, but who would put her in such a state?
A zombie, maybe, who lived in her class, called Spooky Sally.'

Martell Lewis (12)
Heath Park High School

THE CURSE OF THE VAMPIRE

Thunder was striking,
The vampire awoke,
The vampire was thirsty,
The vampire went hunting for flesh.

Vampire went to the graveyard,
There stood the slayer.
The slaying began,
The vampire was sucking and draining the blood.
The slayer grew weaker,
The slayer pulled out a cross.
Vampire disappeared into thin air
And said, 'I'll be back.'

Manjinder Kaur Shihmar (13)
Heath Park High School

THE CURSE OF ALL CURSES

The curse of mystery,
The curse of fear,
The curse of curses.

The curse of murder,
The curse of dreams,
The curse of screams.

The curse that makes your heart pound,
The curse that makes you run for fear,
The curse that makes you run for death,
The curse that makes your heart thud,
The curse that never ends!

Jade Gayle (12)
Heath Park High School

UNTITLED

There are two sides to everything,
Even the future.

We can never be sure
What the future will hold.

Fields of deceased soldiers,
English, French, German,
All nationalities.
Cries of pain deafening my ears.

We can never be sure
What the future will hold.

It was on the news,
Cancer breakthrough!
This will change the world
They said.

We can never be sure
What the future will hold.

A bruise on her face,
Reliving the moment over in her memory,
She shakes with fear,
If only the NSPCC was still around.

We can never be sure
What the future will hold.

Shark hunting banned,
Shark fin soup no longer made,
Sharks free to roam Earth's oceans.

What will the future hold?

Carl Healey (14)
Penn Hall School

INCREDIBLE AGE MACHINE

In 3000 AD
I invented the
Incredible age machine.
5, 4, 3, 2, 1
There go the old women,
One by one.
Fifty-four,
Twenty-nine,
Ten and one.

Now for the lads,
Rocking robots can't be bad.
Beware, beware,
These men were ten . . .
And now who knows.

Paul Hannaford (14)
Penn Hall School

FUTURAMA

It was a dark, dark night,
I looked up at the stars,
It was so extraordinary . . .
A sudden flash of light
Swallowed me whole,
I ended up in a tunnel of light.
I kept on running and running,
I was quivering with fear.
Where am I?
Where will it take me?
When will it end?
Will it end?
Arrrrgh, I'm falling . . .
Bang!
I looked up, I saw a strange robot.
No, please don't hurt me.
A bubble ship flew past me.
Where am I, what year is it?
4005.
You . . . what? You can talk?
Scott, Scott, wake up.
I woke up.
Unfortunately, it was just a dream.

Scott Lloyd (14)
Penn Hall School

FLIGHT TO FLORIDA

I'm cramped,
I'm squashed,
It's a bit of a squeeze,
Not enough room for my knees.
I moan and groan,
I wiggle and fiddle,
But it is worth it in the end.

Christopher Cartwright (13)
Penn Hall School

RACE AGAINST PAIN

Friday night,
Got to get to hospital as fast as we can.
On holiday at the seaside,
Getting lost,
Feeling frustrated . . .
Which way?

Mom is in pain,
Her leg aches.
Crying.
Car swerves right,
It's twelve o'clock at night.

Scrrrr! Goes the car.
I see the sign,
Here at last . . .
Relief.

Simon Jordan (13)
Penn Hall School

My Sister's Baby

Rushing quickly in the car,
Dashing,
Racing.
My brothers are messing about,
They're irritable.
I want to get close,
To hold him.
I'm worried.
Will he be as ugly as a warthog,
Or will he be as handsome as me?

Sam Downing (13)
Penn Hall School

BIRTHDAY JOURNEY

I'm going to the seaside,
It's my birthday treat.
I'm happy,
Excited,
Pleased . . .
I'm going to be fourteen.

Hayley Cresswell (14)
Penn Hall School

THE FUTURE?

I pull down the lever,
A roaring noise,
My futuristic flying car glides
Quietly on the verge to take-off.

In a flash of light
I disappear,
Never to be seen again.

In 4001,
I see robots scurrying like ants
Across the road;
Virtual reality dogs
Appear and fade away,
Like pictures on a computer screen.
People reprogrammed against their will;
Eyes stare
With no expression to be seen,
Unaware of what the future may hold for them.

Shereen Croasdale (15)
Penn Hall School

THE ABSOLUTELY ANYTHING MACHINE

The Absolutely Anything Machine
Goes really fast, like a hurricane.
It talks through the control,
It has the mind of a human being,
It flies like a tornado at 500mph.

The Absolutely Anything Machine
Is like a genie in a bottle.
It grants my every wish.
What shall I wish for?

Harry Shenton (14)
Penn Hall School

HERE I SIT IN MY F1 CAR

Here I sit in my F1 car wondering what it will be like
Speeding around Silverstone . . .

I'm in pole position and we're off,
Building up my speed 30, 50, 70, 90, 110, 130mph.
I take the first bend steady, look at all those
Ferrari fans cheering me on.
Oh no, Hagi Bonfi has just overtaken me,
Then I take a sharp left, with my wheels skidding everywhere
I think it's time for a pit stop.
As I pull in, I can see all the mechanics waiting.
'Hurry up!' I shout, as they try their hardest to change my tyres quickly,
Seven seconds, eight, nine, at last I'm ready to start again.
I build up my speed slowly as I drive out of the pit lane,
Then it's onto the home straight.
I can see Hagi Bonfi just in front of me,
90, 110, 130, 150, 170, 190, 210, I'm catching him up.
Five, four, three, two, one, I have. I've done it, *yes, I've won!*

Third place goes to Philip Menda of Spain,
Second place goes to Hagi Bonfi of Chile,
And first place goes to Richard Amos of England,
And with that, he's awarded the 9052 Championship
Driver of the Year.

Richard Amos (14)
Penn Hall School

THE MOON

On a cold night, tucked up in bed,
I looked at the silver circle in the dark, night sky.

A wondrous sight, the sun's reflecting light
Making it bright.

And the craters making shadows across the rough surface,
Looking like features on a happy face.

Kimberley Croxall (11)
Perton Middle School

ARE WE TREATING EARTH WITH RESPECT?

Look at the planet, our planet Earth,
Look at the way we treat it, look at what it looks like.
Do we really want our Earth to be used like a scrap yard?
Are we maintaining our planet by using parts of it like a factory?
Are we respecting God's creation, our own home?

Look at the children on Earth,
Some of them aren't being treated like humans,
They are being used as slaves,
Children are meant to have freedom, but they aren't getting it.
Some are having to suffer cruelty, pain and hunger,
Why don't we give them a chance to lead a proper life,
A good life, like the rest of us?
Why don't we give them a chance to have a life
Free of hunger, pain and cruelty?
They deserve the right to drink water and eat food
That won't kill them.

How are we treating the animals on this planet?
Are we helping them to survive by setting down traps
To injure and kill them?
Is killing them and selling their fur the right way to treat them?
We should be taking care of them and letting them lead their lives,
In the same way we would wish to lead ours.

Let's try to learn how to treat Earth with a little respect.

Jack Harmer (12)
Perton Middle School

WHAT IS A BROTHER?

A brother is . . .
Silly,
Loving,
Caring,
Sometimes a pain,
Naughty,
Daring,
Has a fight,
Gets into trouble,
Sometimes he gets muddled,
Sometimes forgiving,
Depends what you've done.
A brother's lovely,
Just think about it.

Emma Clarke (11)
Perton Middle School

SPRING

Birds sing, I glance at the trees that wave
And the daffodils that dance.
Spurting flowers, a gentle breeze,
The leaves are scuffling on the trees.

Eggs are laid, lambs are born,
Bluebells blossom early in the morn.
The bright, fiery sun flickers in the sky,
And butterflies flutter, way up high.

Spring says, 'Good morning,' winter says, 'Good night.'
Shadows cast and form when objects don't hit the light.
Grass fresh and green, horizon in the deep,
Spring suddenly awakens from its long lasting sleep.

Kirenjeet Bunger (12)
Perton Middle School

IMAGINE

Imagine yourself as a leaf, floating high,
Imagine yourself as a leaf, floating in the great blue sky.

Imagine yourself as a lion, leaping through the air,
Imagine yourself as a lion, leaping from here to there.

Imagine yourself as a memory, never fading away,
Imagine yourself as a memory, there as a reminder, every day.

Rebecca Lomas (11)
Perton Middle School

MY DOG GEORGIE

My dog's coat is brown and curly,
She's mischievous, playful and quite burly.

She barks to let us know her needs,
She plays in the garden among the leaves.

She follows my mum wherever she goes,
Sniffing the air with her damp, black nose.

She bounds around, her ears flap about,
She's having fun, of that there's no doubt.

All has gone quiet, we take a peep,
She's all run out and fast asleep.

Liam McWilliams (11)
Perton Middle School

WHAT IS PEACE?

No fighting,
No war,
Just peace
Forever more.
No disagreements,
No fighting,
No terrorism,
Just kindness.
No weapons,
No bombing,
No fighter planes
Ruling the skies.
Let the world unite,
Let no one fight.
The wrong should go,
The right should show.

Sarah Collisson (11)
Perton Middle School

LITTLE BROTHERS

My little brother is a mastermind at plotting,
His plan is to be quite annoying.
My brother is a machine used for destroying,
My brother uses his special powers of pestering
And his stealth power of sneaking.

Sometimes I think my little brother does not care,
Sometimes I think his mind is floating in the air.
Sometimes he fills me with greatest despair,
The good thing is, he is easy to scare.

But in the end, a brother is a brother,
So we should take care of one another.

Nicholas Samuels (11)
Perton Middle School

WHAT IS SNOW?

Snow is white
And as bright as a light.
Snow is cold
And can turn into ice.

Snow is fun
When in a sleigh run.
Snow is sad,
It can make one bad.

Snow is rough,
It can be quite tough.
Snow is sleek,
Like a penguin's beak.

Amy Gill (11)
Perton Middle School

WHAT IS?

What is a friend? Someone who's there,
Full of kindness and handfuls of care.
What is a parent? Someone who loves,
Full of forgiveness, kisses and hugs.
What is a boyfriend? Someone charming,
Lovable, cuddly, calls me his darling.
What is a family? People who share,
Who I go home to with my nightmares.
What is a home? Secure and safe,
Cosy, warm, my very own place!
What is my life? Complicated but true,
So many high goals for me and for you.

Hannah Rogers (12)
Perton Middle School

WHAT ARE THE SEASONS?

The seasons are changes in weather,
Some people like them, some people hate them.

Spring is the first,
Baby lambs in the field,
Daffodils swaying in the breeze,
Buds of blossom ready to burst.

Summer is the second,
Green leaves on the trees,
Hopefully it will be warm,
When the sunshine beckons.

The seasons are changes in weather,
Some people like them, some people hate them.

Autumn is the third,
Leaves of red and golden yellow,
The harvest comes in, fortunes untold,
Song of the summer birds now unheard.

Winter is the fourth,
The branches on the trees bare, no leaves,
As children build snowmen,
Blowing in my hair is the cold wind from the north.

The seasons are changes in weather,
Some people like them, some people hate them.

Hayley Cox (11)
Perton Middle School

What Is Life?

Life is . . .
Joyful,
Sad,
Good,
Bad,
Fun,
Boring,
Unfair,
Depressing,
Happy,
Exciting,
Selfish,
Mad,
Frightening,
Scary,
Meaningful,
Unforgettable.
That's what life is.

Rebecca Burns (11)
Perton Middle School

LIFE

Life is . . .

Fun,
An adventure,
Boring,
Exciting,
Unforgettable,
Hardworking,
Challenging,
Happy,
Sad,
Sometimes dangerous,
Scary,
Meaningful,
Nervous,
Joyful.
That's what life is!

Natalie Mason (11)
Perton Middle School

TERRORISM

Terrorism is cruel and mean,
It will make us very keen
To destroy this horrid thing.

Death and destruction
Are parts of war.
We will argue evermore?

Many die for religion,
On purpose they kill,
People are murdered
By these terrorism makers.

Children become orphans
When their parents die,
But they will never forget
Their painful cry.

Explosions are caused
By bombs and more,
Can we ever live in
Peace?

Amie Farrington (11)
Perton Middle School

WHAT IS WAR?

Bombs and missiles raining down,
Blasting buildings all around.
People huddle together in fright,
Praying they'll make it through the night.

The sky lights up with a golden glow,
Illuminating the ruins down below.
Streets eerily empty, there's no one around,
They're all in the shelter, down below ground.

Death and destruction all around,
Suffering and heartbreak abound.
Twisted metal flies through the air,
Flak jackets and helmets everywhere.

Lost lives, lost loves, what's it all for,
This insane action that we call war?

David Barber (11)
Perton Middle School

WHAT IS A MUMMY?

What is a mummy?

A person who gave birth,
Loving,
Caring,
Giving,
Generous,
Considerate,
Trustworthy,
Fair,
Courteous,
Kind,
Helpful,
Thoughtful.

Anne Renton (11)
Perton Middle School

What Is Autumn?

Autumn is windy, cold and breezy,
Where leaves are found
Floating to the ground.
Why is the sky so cloudy and bright,
Which brings pouring down so much happiness and light?

We watch trees swaying in the breeze,
Down towards the cold winter nights.
But it brings happiness and spring and the flying of all the kites.
Why does autumn have to be so cold?
It's probably because it's near winter and everyone's so bold.

But what does it matter? We love autumn leaves
And how they fall off the trees.
Although summer's gone, don't be so sad,
You have autumn now and you should be glad.

Emma Wisniewski (11)
Perton Middle School

QUESTIONS ABOUT EARTH

At night,
When the moon was shining bright,
I lay on my bed
Then thought and said,

'When you're young,
You don't understand
What's happening on Earth,
So you ask questions.

The Earth, is it peaceful?
The Earth, is it harmful?
What's happening in nature?
Are there any wars?
Where? Why?'

As I lay on my bed,
I wondered . . .

The Earth contains diseases,
Innocent people getting killed,
Why?
But then,
Babies being born,
Dewdrops on fresh grass in the morning,
Peace!

What is the Earth?
Why is it here?
Why are we here?
How was Earth made?
If God made Earth,
Who made God?

So many questions,
So few answers.
Can you answer them?

Rebecca Smith (11)
Perton Middle School

WAR!

War is a symbol of hatred,
Dominance, greed and suffering.
Crash, bang, boom,
Injured, crying, dying, dead!
Not coping, suicidal.

War, guns, bombs, grief,
100,000 in peril, 7,000 dead, 2,000 heroes,
But the war heroes do not want
To remember their battles.

Not for their country or their lives,
But for their peace,
Which remains forever trapped
Within their own sad and lonely conscience.

Joshua Giddings (11)
Perton Middle School

WAR POEM

Fighting is bad and it is sad.
Lots of people die and get shot, bleed and cry.
Some say it is good, some say it is bad,
All I think of is blood.

The bombs are dropping, people are staring,
In a glance, I see someone in a trance.
Far away a sign will say,
'Welcome to the valley of death.'

Mathew Gough (12)
Perton Middle School

A WAR POEM

A crash, a bang, the war has begun.
Thunder, lightning, they all run.
Charging towards the daylight,
But can't find it, they're still in the night.

Bombs are going off, with the sound of screaming,
All of the people in a trance, like they're dreaming.
They hope that it's over and that they've won,
But now they're glad it's all done.

Olivia Cleland (12)
Perton Middle School

WAR SOLDIER

Many people lost their lives, and many had wives.
Their wives were mourning, after being left with no warning.
The family has lost a life.

Will you go to war, or will you run away?
Will you kill the enemy, or live another day?
Will you make your mother proud, or make your father sad?
But if you do not go to war, it's the Germans who'll be glad.

Hannah Jeffs (12)
Perton Middle School

WAR

Soldiers sobbed silently
When gunshots violently banged
With puddles of blood
And bodies asleep
As they ran from base to base
With lights hovering above.
Rest in peace, rest in peace,
Instead of just dark nights,
Dark days all week.
Can you picture the men,
So weak, so weak.
Rest in peace, rest in peace,
Where the body did rot,
Now is not a part of
The enemy's land.
'It is our land.'
They breathe in our English ashes,
They tread on our English soil,
So we will never forget
The death that was met
In that fighting field.

Kathryn Rogers (12)
Perton Middle School

A WAR POEM

Nations' armies fighting back,
Right here for attack.
A bang, a crash,
The bullets dash.
Soldiers shout,
Ill-tempered lout.
Defending their country lost,
They will have to pay a cost!

Jenny Tyrer (13)
Perton Middle School

ZODIAC

The next time you look at the stars,
Look a bit closer and then,
You'll see
The sky is a blanket
That covers the truth,
But underneath if you look,
Lie stories, tales and amazing things.

The tales of life,
The tales of death,
The coming of fortune
The zodiac brings.

A curious Aquarius gives
Peace to your life,
Or a cautious Capricorn may
Give you strength.
A courageous Aries might
Bring you luck.

So the next time
You look at the stars,
Look a bit closer
And see what they bring
To you . . .

Emma Marston (14)
St Edmund's RC School

THE TWELVE SIGNS OF THE ZODIAC

Aries has energy, enthusiasm and is courageous,
Taurus has a good memory, though can be very clumsy.
Gemini is charming, sensitive and generous,
Cancer is sympathetic, but also moody.
Leo is the lion, daring and cheerful,
Virgo is charming, honest and nervous.
Libra is lazy, nevertheless truthful,
Scorpio is cautious, as well as courageous,
Sagittarius is sporty, honest and happy,
Capricorn is arrogant, cruel and gloomy.
Aquarius is happy, truthful and friendly,
Pisces is warm, though likes to throw away money.
They are the twelve star signs throughout the year,
So which end is yours nearer to, the start or the rear?

James Turner (13)
St Edmund's RC School

ZODIAC POEM

I like to read my horoscope,
So I know what the day will bring.
I always start the day in hope
That perhaps today I'll sing,
But with a sign like Gemini,
My mind is in two halves,
Today's not the day to sing,
Instead I've changed my mind.

Jennifer McHugh (13)
St Edmund's RC School

ZODIAC

We start to look at the stars up above,
Capricorn, Aries and Leo.
The wonder that they bring to life,
Taurus my special sign.

The bull of strength, courage and love,
Of course that sign is correct!
My family is of four different signs,
Taurus, Capricorn, Libra and Virgo.

A mixture of the stars up above,
Sometimes seen or well hidden.
The meanings lie in their complexion of light,
All so very clear.

Some of anger, strength and loyalty,
Some of passion and joy.
All so calm, clear and bold
With many of their stories yet to be told.

Laura Ciancimino (13)
St Edmund's RC School

THE SIGNS OF THE ZODIAC

T   he signs of the zodiac are mysterious things,
H   elping us find what the future will bring.
E   very night in the sky the stars shine bright,

S   hooting through the chilling moonlight.
I   n the heavens above, the signs slowly form,
G   oing away when the night turns to morn.
N   o sight more mysterious
S   een with my eyes.

O   ver the moon the bright stars fly,
F   rom east to west across the heavens they go.

T   hat trail of light that disappears so slow,
H   aving gone in the morning.
E   very night they come back,

Z   ipping across the sky so black,
O   ut of the sky they come,
D   own with the darkness, then out comes the sun.
I   n the end of the day
A   nd at the end of the night, the signs will be there,
C   learly in the moonlight.

Rhys Thomas (13)
St Edmund's RC School

THE SIGNS OF THE ZODIAC

The signs of the zodiac high in the sky,
A cluster of stars with Earth nearby.
Your horoscope depends on when you were born,
Could it be Cancer, Leo, or maybe Capricorn?
People believe the future is told in the stars,
In the stars between Neptune and Mars.
You can see Leo let out a courageous roar,
In just a couple of stars hanging over the seashore.
When we look to the stars, everything's fine,
In this wonderful universe, which is yours and mine.

Danielle Pritz (14)
St Edmund's RC School

MY ZODIAC FAMILY

My mom's a Leo and she roars like a lion,
She's daring and loyal,
With ambitions to fulfil.
It seems her star sign really fits the bill.
My dad is a Pisces and his hobby is to fish,
He's warm and lovable,
And romantic through and through.
It seems the stars work for him too.
Now we come to my older sister
Who is very good natured,
She can be happy, honest and intelligent,
Sporty and gregarious,
What a surprise, she's a Sagittarius.
My brother loves football and supports Man U,
He can be lazy but also kind and truthful,
Yes, he's a Libra and very well balanced,
He's a little boy with many talents.
There's only me left in my family of five,
I'm charming, sensitive and generous.
Gemini is my June-born sign,
And that's the zodiac family of mine!

Fiona Woodhead (13)
St Edmund's RC School

ZODIAC

Zodiac are the signs that fill our sky with light,
Every star is like a person's soul,
They burn fiercely and look down at us.
They keep the Earth bright and
Cast out darkness' shadow.
They stretch over the entire universe,
Filling every galaxy, even in their darkest corners.
Stars of the zodiac are infinite,
They never fade away or vanish without trace.
They shine for a millennia, all different shapes and sizes.
They form the constellations that appear
In our beautiful, dark night sky,
And when you are lonely at night,
You can look up at the stars and let
Their brightness and signs overwhelm you.

Matt Kulyna (13)
St Edmund's RC School

ZODIAC POEM

Z   eus, god of war,
O f Virgo's origin,
D o you agree with what you're like?
I   s Taurus patient?
A ries proud?
C an we believe such cant?

Is it worth it to rant and rave
About silly pictures that tell us how we behave?
Just because I was born in September,
How does that make me like work, be selfish
And other things I can't remember?
You are what you are, you do what you do,
You can believe all this, it's up to you.

Theo Neumann (14)
St Edmund's RC School

ZODIAC

Z   is for Zeus, the king of the gods,
O   is for orbits of the planets above,
D   is for dates of years and months,
I   is for the identity we get from our stars,
A   is for air, one of the elements of our charts,
C   is for curiosity we fulfil by reading our stars.

Philippa Hedges (13)
St Edmund's RC School

ZODIAC

Night falls like waterfalls,
Splashing stars around the sky,
Shooting stars go zooming by,
All forming an amazing painting.
The patterns influence us all,
Gemini or Leo, Taurus or Scorpio,
From the day you were born,
Your fate is decided.
So,
Banker, baker, soldier or sailor,
The future is foggy, uncertain and unclear.
So look to the stars, the future is there.
Which character are you to be?
Let fate decide, won't you?

Mark Taylor (13)
St Edmund's RC School

ZODIAC

The signs of the Zodiac,
Twelve mark the skies,
Each come together
To amaze unique eyes.

Virgo is the lady,
Caring and true,
Libras are balanced,
Scorpions sting you.

Sagittarius can pierce
With bow and arrow,
Capricorn's the goat,
With patience, very narrow.

Aquarius, the refresher,
Goddess, gentle and fair,
Pisces the fish
Comes forth to take care.

Leo the beast,
Crowned prince in seeking,
Cancer that plagues you
In a manner of speaking.

Aries, the ram,
Taurus, the bull,
Gemini's a leader,
Can sometimes be dull.

The signs of the Zodiac,
Twelve mark the skies,
Each come together
To amaze unique eyes.

Michaela Mincher (14)
St Edmund's RC School

ZODIAC

Z odiac means the signs and symbols
O f the jet-black sky.
D eep and far away in the emptiness of space.
I   n the stars is where people rely on their futures
A nd where they try to find answers to all their problems,
C hecking every day, putting their hope and faith in
     the signs of the Zodiac.

Arron Jones (14)
St Edmund's RC School

ZODIAC

Z odiac, zodiac, what's your prediction for this week?
O minous, typical, optimistic or smashing?
D isturb my daily boring life please, sometime,
I f only you could predict money for me,
A nd luck or success or fame.
C hallenge yourself zodiac, my horoscopes say all the same.

Laura McBrien (13)
St Edmund's RC School

PRINCESS NIGHT

Dressed in midnight blue clothes,
Well protected from all her foes,
Her beautiful features make you gaze,
Even Day does upon her gaze.

The planets adorn her dress,
Anyone who saw it would confess
How the zodiac sparkles in her hair
And is far more pretty than anyone could wear.

Twinkling silently, do her tears flow,
Tears as bright as the stars' glow,
Waiting for Chronos to let her go,
Waiting for escape to show.

Princess Night silently waits,
Weaving, intertwining fates,
Stirring deep into people's lust and passions,
Hard she works and hard she fashions.

She labours long and hard
And for time and space she does guard
The gateways to Heaven and Hell
And makes sure no one will of them tell.

As long as a piece of string,
As long as Earth does give spring,
For as long as eternity will last,
She will guard Present, Future and Past.

She is waiting for her long lost love,
When she can join him far above.
When time will end, when all's vanished,
When she can return from being banished.

Banished to a lifetime up with the stars,
Decorated with Jupiter, Venus and Mars,
Yearning for her lover, yearning for his kiss,
How much longer will she be denied bliss?

Sam Ryan (13)
St Edmund's RC School

ZODIAC

Proud and honest, loyal and true,
Lazy, secretive, gloomy and cruel,
Each sign is unique - just for you,
Scorpio or Pisces, which one is you?

Leo the lion, proud, loyal and daring,
Gemini the twins, two-faced but charming.

They give insight into your life,
They tell us what you're really like.
Aries, Virgo, Cancer too,
Each one will tell us all about you!

Leanne Galloway (13)
St Edmund's RC School

ZODIAC

Way up in the stars where nobody can see,
All the way up in the skies,
Beyond the sun, moon and sea,
That is where the Zodiac lies.
You may read in your horoscope what is ahead,
Into the future so far.
'You will have a disappointment in love,' it said,
Or 'You'll be famous, a model, a star.'
An arrow, a lion, all sorts of signs
To represent your mood.
As a Leo, I'm ambitious, cheerful and kind,
But big-headed and a show-off. (How rude!)
My horoscope - I don't know whether it's true,
But look for yourself and maybe you'll do.

Nicola Banyard (13)
St Edmund's RC School

ZODIAC

Why does everyone follow the stars?
It's not like we're from Pluto or Mars.
Eagerly waiting for the paperboy
So you can read what you're meant to be doing, what joy!
It's like the weather forecast that's never right,
Why should everyone read this stuff? I'll put up a fight.
Patterns in the night sky
Will determine whether you live or die,
And after all, it's easy money
For the stargazers who think it's funny
To exploit normal people, like me.

James Brewerton (13)
St Edmund's RC School

SAYS THE VOICE OF THE STARS

Z ones of space will be churning to make more
    friction in our lives - says the voice of the stars.
O rbits of the planets can cause jealousy or in
    some cases, violence - says the voice of the stars.
D ivided into twelve signs to represent you and
    your ever-changing life - says the voice of the stars.
I   am Aquarius, lashing out because of Saturn's rings
    is what I'm doing - says the voice of the stars.
A chieving and playing the good days and beating the
    bad days is success - says the voice of the stars.
C ancer, Leo, Virgo, Libra, Scorpio, Sagittarius,
    Capricorn, Aquarius, Pisces, Aries, Taurus and Gemini
    is what we are - says the voice of the stars.

Carl Watkins (13)
St Edmund's RC School

THE HOROSCOPE CHILDREN

January's child is water-born,
Aquarius your star sign,
Of trouble I must warn.

Pisces child is born like a fish,
Sports you are good at,
May life bring you bliss.

Aries, be cautious,
There are problems ahead,
Someone could say something that shouldn't be said.

Taurus calm down, the air is now clear,
Don't be reluctant,
Something is near.

Gemini twins can't find their ground,
You'll need to spark up,
Be ready to pound.

Cancer the crab, it's up to your trust,
Friends need your help,
Therefore you must.

Leos are lions, lucky as you are,
Something's unsure of,
The answer comes from afar.

Virgos child, without worry,
Don't feel too laid back,
You'll need to scurry.

Libra's well balanced, but cowardly and vain,
Don't be too harsh
Or you may not gain.

Scorpio's child is cautious but proud,
Someone disliked
Stands out from the crowd.

Sagittarius' child, clumsy but kind,
It's your determination,
Make up your mind.

Last on the list, Capricorn's child,
Things will become rough,
Be patient and mild.

Emily Griffiths (14)
St Edmund's RC School

DISASTER STRIKES!

America was peaceful
Until today.
The Twin Towers fell
And caused dismay.

The world feels the sorrow
That America feels,
The broken-hearted,
And families parted.

The time was 9:02,
When the sorrows unwound,
People cried
When the Twin Towers fell to the ground.

People were upset
And some still are,
To see their families die
And become far.

Our school
Had a moment of silence,
We thought about the
Thousands of people that had died.

My last thought was
World War III.
Please make this nightmare end
So that I can't see.

Cassie Morgan (12)
The King's School

DISASTER STRIKES AGAIN!

America was peaceful
Until the day
The Twin Towers fell
And caused dismay.

Broken-hearted,
Families parted,
Sadness started.

Innocent people lost their lives,
Families cried in almighty despair.
Husbands searched for wives,
All the while pulling out their hair.

Broken-hearted,
Families parted,
Sadness started.

Curiosity astounded me,
Questions I asked my mom.
She was not filled with glee,
I was scared of what was going to happen to me.

Broken-hearted,
Shall never be mended.

Families parted,
Shall never be united.

Sadness started,
Will never end.

Gemma Astbury (11)
The King's School

CRIES OF AMERICA

Self-sacrifice, what a terrible thing,
Suicide, to life they don't cling.
Honour, to defend their race,
Afghanistan, at the moment what a terrible place.

Shocked people everywhere sigh.
Children, for their lost parents they cry.
Lost, somewhere in the rubble they hide,
Shouting, firemen try to find.

I feel so frightened, so helpless,
So utterly scared.
My disgust
I want to declare.

So many opinions I have,
So many views,
But which are right,
How do I choose?

War on terrorism Bush has declared,
People everywhere, scared.
Tragedy as the Twin Towers fall,
Rescuers, to people they call.

War,
It has now started.
Families,
Will all be parted.
I'm so sick of the human race.
Argh! Get me out of this place!

Stephanie Hickman (12)
The King's School

AMERICA

Families torn apart,
Thousands of people with broken hearts.
All were saddened, all have cried,
But a different story across the tides.
Watched by hundreds on TV,
Shocked and outraged by what they see.
People rejoicing at what they have lost,
Gladly celebrating at their cost.
Now war may be on the agenda for America,
Only the soldiers can mend her.
Already waiting in the wings,
Dreading the time the commander sings,
World War III hopefully not to be!
Now we remember those who died,
Commemorating those who tried,
But again the sun has shone,
And now life must go on.

Jessica Labhart (12)
The King's School

BIRTHDAYS

Birthdays, happy days,
Cakes and presents arriving,
Birthdays, happy days.

Celebrating you,
Meeting people while smiling,
Surprises for you.

Music is loud,
People all around dancing,
All celebrating you.

Tina Willington (15)
Wednesfield High School

THE SUN

Sun glows bright one day,
High up in the clear, blue sky.
It burns brightly all day through,
Hope it never ends, do you?

Adam Leslie (16)
Wednesfield High School

FEELINGS

I'm getting fed up with everything,
I'm feeling really blue,
Is someone going to help me,
And is it going to be you?

I'm glad you're around,
You silly old clown,
Your laughing and giggling
Makes me happy all year round.

Rachel Badger (15)
Wednesfield High School

UNDER THE BED

I creep downstairs
And open the fridge
And eat all your food
And watch TV
And hear the door knock,
One, two, three.

I creep back upstairs
And kiss you goodnight
And look at the clock,
Tick-tock.

I look out of the window
And see all the stars
And say, 'I wish I
Was in my car.'

So I finally go to sleep,
So there I am,
The creeper under the bed.

Luke Leedham (11)
Wednesfield High School

LOVE

Love is an emotion
That can be filled with hurt and pain.
You can love someone so badly,
It could make you go insane.

Love can be sweet, kind and unselfish,
Love can stand up to the test.
When you find someone trustworthy,
Love can be the very best.

Love is blind, it comes and goes
And sometimes hard to find,
But some unlucky people
Never get the chance to know.

There are different kinds of love,
Like for a brother or your friends.
Love doesn't always go so perfect,
And with tears it finally ends.

Sophia Thompson (15)
Wednesfield High School

HALLOWE'EN

Witches, wizards and pumpkin pies,
Stay together side by side.

Vampires, Frankenstein and wcrewolves too,
Make the party a really spooky do.

Werewolves howl and vampires bite,
Frankenstein likes to come out at the dead of night!

Mummies, zombies, ghosts and fiends,
All make ghastly screeching screams.

Mummies in bandages and zombies in goo,
Ghosts and fiends away at the do.

Laura Badger (11)
Wednesfield High School

HALLOWE'EN

It was the biggest pumpkin I had ever seen,
I knew it was the one we must have for Hallowe'en.
I took it home the day before,
But almost got stuck going through the door.

Guests at the party will include witches and wizards in tall,
                                          pointed hats,
Ghosts, werewolves and vampires with bats.
In my black, swirling skirt and my best pointed hat,
No other witch will look finer than that.

With a pumpkin so grand and a broom in my hand,
It makes me so proud to be here.
Footsteps up the drive signify
That the guests are coming near.

Natalie Harney (11)
Wednesfield High School

SQUIRREL

It has come on a warm summer breeze,
Autumn is here, that is certainly clear.
I know now that I must prepare for a long, long sleep,
While you and your friends play around at my feet,
Making piles of leaves, then kicking them up,
After that you will make balls of a cold, white, icy mix.
Then you throw them at each other and play other tricks.
In three months I will awake,
From a quiet, peaceful slumber.
Until then, goodnight.

Danielle Pearce (11)
Wednesfield High School

SOMETIMES I AM . . .

Sometimes I am angry,
Sometimes I am sad,
Sometimes I am sorry,
Sometimes I feel strong,
Sometimes I feel weak.

Sometimes I am an angel,
Sometimes I am a little devil,
Sometimes I am funny and make people laugh,
Sometimes I am miserable, others wonder why.

Sometimes I am happy,
Sometimes I am unhappy,
Sometimes I am lazy,
Sometimes I am helpful,
Sometimes I am crazy.

Kishan Patel (11)
Wednesfield High School

JUNK FOOD

Candy is sweet,
Chocolates are smooth,
Ice cream is runny
And also is honey.

McDonald's has Happy Meals,
Delicious and fun,
If you take it away you can eat it on the run.
Hot dogs are yummy to fit in your tummy.

Crisps are crunchy and fit in your mouth,
I like Walkers, especially salt and vinegar.
Leave my crisp alone you naughty Gary Lineker!
Junk food is good,
Junk food is nice,
But junk food
Is my only vice!

Natalie Powell (11)
Wednesfield High School

GHOST

Spooky and weird noises,
I hear freaking me out,
I wonder if I could speak
To whatever it was?
One night I was going to sleep,
It was sitting at the bottom of my bed,
I screamed at the ghost and
The ghost never came back again.

Jodie Emery (11)
Wednesfield High School

SCHOOLDAYS

It was a hot summer's day,
I wanted to go out and play,
But instead I had to go to school,
Now that isn't very cool.
I suppose it teaches us a lot,
But sometimes I don't get the plot.

I think today I have PE,
Then later, I have RE.

Now I'm heading off to school,
As I said, that's not so cool.
All of a sudden, I get to the gates,
Now all I've got to do is wait

To have a horrid day at school.

Jenny Thompson (11)
Wednesfield High School

A VOICE IN MY HEAD

A voice in my head
Shows me things withered and dead.
As I wake up in bed,
So heavy is my head.

So cold is my bed,
Since it is autumn,
Leaves are falling from
Some old, dying trees.

As I walk around the dying trees,
With the fresh air and the cold breeze,
I hear the voice in my head,
'It is too late, they are already dead.'

As I fear that I have done wrong,
I think of the trees, their roots so strong,
And the leaves that were so young,
In their last seconds they clung and clung.

Christopher Caddick (11)
Wednesfield High School

WALK IN THE WOODS

The lights flashing on and off,
Rustling of trees,
Owls crying,
That's why I don't walk in the woods.

The trees the shape of ghosts,
Moon shining bright,
Making you afraid,
That's why I don't walk in the woods.

The darkness makes you shiver,
Can't see your hand,
Sounds of ghosts,
That's why I don't walk in the woods.

Sharna Sinclair (11)
Wednesfield High School

SPIDERS

Spiders can be creepy,
Spiders can be small,
Spiders can seem very big
When climbing up your wall.

Sometimes they are quick,
Sometimes they are slow,
Some of them are hard to find,
Because you don't know where they go.

Spiders can be hairy,
Spiders can be bald,
Spiders may have long legs
And some have really short.

Spiders like the bathtub,
Spiders like the home,
Spiders like their freedom,
So leave the damn things alone.

Adam Stokley (11)
Wednesfield High School

DARK AT NIGHT

It was dark at night
And a light shone bright.
I gazed up at the stars
And I carried on up a hill.
I saw a scary reflection
Of someone or something.

Sarah Tedstill (11)
Wednesfield High School

IT'S SCOTT DOBIE

When the ball hits the goal,
It's not Shearer or Cole,
It's Scott Dobie.

When the ball hits the net,
You can bet it's a shot
By Scott Dobie.

When Neil Clement takes a corner,
Scott heads the ball
And you can bet
He's the scorer.

Scott Ratcliffe (11)
Wednesfield High School

PETS

Miss Animal has lots of pets.
She has a dog called Fairy,
Who is very, very hairy.
A cat called Pies,
Who has big, orange eyes.
Sally the rat,
Who lives in a hat.
A cow called Moo,
Who ate a shoe.
Pork the porcupine,
Who likes to drink wine.
A rabbit called Skip,
Who is very hip.
An owl called Poo,
Who never stops saying tu-whit, tu-whoo,
And a pig called Hog,
Who is five times the size of a big dog.
I've always wanted a pet like Miss Animal's,
But I'm stuck with my brother.

Joanne Leslie (11)
Wednesfield High School

MY RAINBOW POEM

Red is the colour of liquid blood,
Red is the colour of my brother's hair,
Red is the strawberry just been picked,
And red is a cherry just been licked.

Yellow is some custard in a tin,
Also yellow is a banana skin.
Yellow is melting butter
And yellow is always a daffodil's colour.

Pink is the colour of a strawberry sherbet,
Pink is the colour of my sister's lipstick,
Pink is the colour I go when I feel silly,
Pink is the colour of a special birthday bow.

Green is the colour of fresh, green grass,
Green is the colour of leaves shaking in the wind,
Also, green is a stem surviving.
Green is the colour you are before you're sick.

Orange is a beautiful colour,
Orange is rusty leaves in the autumn,
Orange is also a fruit grown in a country where the sun shines bright,
Orange is an orange, which of course is orange.

Blue is ice,
Blue is cold,
Blue is the ocean that crashes on the shore
And blue is the colour of the deep, blue sea.

Charlotte Court (11)
Wednesfield High School

KEVIN AND SADIE

Catholic and Protestant,
Boy and girl
Find each other
In Ireland.

Kevin and Sadie
Fall in love
In Ireland,
In Belfast.

Kevin and Sadie
Have a secret,
Kept from the families,
About love.

Kevin and Sadie
Go out together,
To Bangor,
On the bus.

Surinder Kaur (13)
Wednesfield High School

PROTESTANTS AND CATHOLICS

There is fighting in the street,
People running, hear their feet.
Guns are firing in the night,
I can't wait until it's light.

When I wake, I look outside,
Shops on fire, hide, hide, hide!
I go outside to look around,
People dead on the ground.

I'm walking round and round
And then I hear an unusual sound.
I look up above just to see
A fighter jet looking at me.

When it's gone I wipe my brow,
Just to hear a scream and cry.
I see a woman crawling towards me,
Her legs were chopped off at the knee.

Anton Smith (14)
Wednesfield High School

IRELAND

I   reland is intimidated by war,
R   omance is in the air, danger is getting closer,
E   veryone is fighting for their religion,
L   ove is in the heart of Ireland,
A   nger is in the air because of people's religion,
N   o one is happy in Northern Ireland,
D   anger is everywhere for everyone.

Jordon Mohan (13)
Wednesfield High School

ACROSS THE BARRICADES

Bombs go off everywhere,
People stand in horror and stare.
People watch victims fall,
As bombs shake pictures on the walls.
Blood everywhere you can see,
It is surely not the place to be,
But Kevin and Sadie stand on Cave Hill
As people fight with all their will.
But it all starts from one problem.
When their families see them,
Together, hand in hand,
Mothers disgusted, fathers mad,
Cos one's Protestant, the other Catholic,
As they walk to Cave Hill with families feeling sick.

Keri Clarke (13)
Wednesfield High School

TWO SIDES TO DEATH

Danger,
    Anger,
        Violence,
            Hate,
What else will come next?
    Unhappiness is what surrounds this place,
        Not love, happiness, or out of fear.

War, they called it,
    But people still find,
        Love but maybe
            With the opposite side.

Stay out of the way of danger,
    They will show all of their anger
        Straight onto you
            Even if you don't agree
                With what they do.

Danielle Williams (13)
Wednesfield High School

THE DARK DAYS

Dark days,
Dark weeks,
Dark months
And maybe years.
There's bombing everywhere,
Dead bodies scattered all over the place
In the dark, black streets.
You can hear screaming from adults and children,
Gunshots everywhere you go,
You can see corner men on foot,
Causing dangerous scares.
Why does it have to be us?

Nicholas Harley (13)
Wednesfield High School

TOMORROW, PLEASE DON'T COME!

Two victims of a war,
They know their lives are in danger,
But their bravery to stick together is unreal.
She is Protestant, he is a Catholic.

Her father is in the Orange Lodge,
Her mother a slave at home,
They don't agree with what she's doing.

His mother, a parent of eight, another on the way,
His father at work all day,
Expects his tea on the table when he gets in.

But outside,
Bombardments of army soldiers
Running through the streets,
Bombs going off,
People's body parts splattered up the walls,
Grieving parents as their children get killed,
Roaming the streets.
Bomb attacks, shop fires, families torn apart.

Two people deeply in love,
Bravery, courage, danger,
Possibility of getting killed.
He has already been beaten up,
'Traitor, traitor,' they called him,
Beat him black and blue.
What was he going to do?

Caroline Jones (13)
Wednesfield High School

ACROSS THE BARRICADES

As bombs explode, parts of bodies fall.
Blood everywhere, all over the floor,
The floor decorated with blood and body parts.
Guns go off, the clattering and thundering,
They scare the people off.
Danger everywhere, people hide,
Some people fight.
War between Catholic and Protestant,
There is hate for each other, no one cares
People get hurt,
They think it's not safe
As violence goes on in the streets.
Families and friends get lonely,
They're scared it might be their turn next.
As all this is happening, two youngsters fall in love,
But they're Catholic and Protestant.
The two youngsters care for each other,
They trust each other,
They cannot live without each other.
But their families and friends don't understand.
Romance is everything for them.
They try to get away,
But they get trapped between the barricades,
They cannot go any further.
They have faith in their love,
It ends up in hurt.
As the brutal injuries get worse,
They are separated,
And it ends in tears.

Leena Sandhu (13)
Wednesfield High School

Poem About War In Ireland

Two different religions are fighting,
Catholics and Protestants
People in danger, feel unsafe,
Too much fighting,
Too much unhappiness.

The two religions are separated by barricades,
Too much violence, too much hurt,
Too much hatred, too many bombs,
Families are caring for each other,
No need for this war!

In between the war and fighting,
People are in love,
Trying to be brave, trying to get the courage,
Friends from the two religions are stuck in the middle,
Friends are trying to understand.

Too many bombs, too much death,
Why does it have to be like this?
People hear gunshots, people panicking,
People dying, people getting injured,
No need for this war!

Two people from the religions are in love,
Feeling uneasy, but feeling safe with each other.
Both their families are fighting,
No need for this fighting.
All this hatred. Why?

One of these days there will be peace between them,
We have to wait for that day.
Too much war, too much fighting,
No need for this war.
When will this war stop?

Fay Lander (13)
Wednesfield High School

UNTITLED

Kevin and Sadie are in love,
Kevin and Sadie are up above,
In the sky they will lie
And there so happy, they will start to cry.

In Northern Ireland there is a place called Cave Hill,
Some people fight with all their will.

Bombs, bombs, everywhere,
Bombs, bombs, do not scare.
In the night you will hear a bang,
And after a few minutes they will clang.

Bombs are going off everywhere,
People stop to stand and stare.

Hayley Ingram (13)
Wednesfield High School

IRISH WAR

Love and hate,
Peace and war,
Blood and guts,
Ireland is at war.

Body parts and limbs,
Protestant and Catholic,
Scared people run,
A religious dispute.

Bombs go off,
Gunfire shots,
Brave men go to war,
Will there ever be peace?

Bodies all over the street,
Children have to run to school,
People lose family members,
It has become an everyday thing.

Night-time comes,
There will be peace in my dreams,
Wish the day will never break,
Stay here all my life.

Jennie Lee (14)
Wednesfield High School

PROTESTANTS AND CATHOLICS ARE AT WAR

Protestants and Catholics are at war,
Everybody locks their windows and door.
The sound of bombs and gunfire can be heard,
There's not an animal in sight, not even a bird.

Occasionally the streets are spattered with blood,
While either side think they are doing good.
Once Ireland's land was ever so green,
Now permanently scarred by acts obscene.

Yet again the police sirens wail,
By a bomb that exploded, sent by the mail.
Both sides attack the authorities and fight,
Fires from riots rage on through the night.

The riots in newspapers are read,
Whilst families mourn their dead.
The ground we walk will never be the same,
Ever since the troubles to Ireland came.

Ellen Jones (13)
Wednesfield High School

CONFLICT IN IRELAND

A dark day, a dark month, another dark year.
Terror and conflict on every street corner,
Men on foot
Committing violent scenes.

Bombs,
Firing of machine guns
Amongst the rubble
Lies death of a bloody war.

King Billy looks aloft
At the devastation,
Splattered red walls,
Limbs a-plenty.

Frightened
As loved ones watch,
Afraid of what will come.
'Why us?'

Tom Bartlett (13)
Wednesfield High School

IRELAND . . . THE UGLY SIDE

As I walk home
With fear in my heart,
Walking from the dreaded yard,
I'm worried what might happen.

Gunshots, bombings,
With murders too,
My voice whispers,
'Why am I here?'

I carry on walking,
A body on the side,
My old friend David,
Resting in peace.

I see a girl,
She is like a bell,
Ringing, ringing
In my heart.

Sadie,
With her glistening eyes.
Danger, I sense,
Am I really taking a risk?

Hey, I'm home.
A tap on the shoulder.
Hit, kick, stab!
Blackness!

Jamie Clift (13)
Wednesfield High School

PEOPLE

People are hard to understand.
You say hello by waving your hand,
They do not wave back.
Is there something that you lack?
You feel you're not as good as them,
Never wave back, ever again.
You waved just to be nice,
Don't make that mistake twice.
They always talk about you.

Reena Mehta (15)
Wednesfield High School

THE CLOSING OF THE BARRICADES

The sun comes up as another day dawns,
You hear people rise and their tired yawns,
They know the wars have only just begun,
For people do this just for fun.
Bombs and guns, they all play a part,
As people grieve in their lonely hearts.
Sometimes these fights end in death,
Hatred and unsafe caring makes
Them breathe their last breath.
These people are out to hurt and hate too,
As these kneecapping nightmares
Spread through and through.
These conflicts of bravery turn their faith into danger,
As people pray for their Lord Saviour.
These religions believe in things that aren't right,
Each casts a spell of violence and fright.
Every person wishes for peace to come,
They put their trust in each other,
As they once had done.
Friends and families come together and understandings are made,
As the barricades close in to claim victims from rage.
The courage, the bravery, it makes people cry
When Catholics and Protestants prepare to die.
The compassion in them sets their hearts on fire,
As unhappy people flee as they tire.
The romance makes them tremble with anticipation,
As they stubbornly hold hands and avoid intimidation.
The love they once shared is now back forever,
As Kevin and Sadie abandon Belfast together!

Rachael Walker (14)
Wednesfield High School

TIGER

Stealthily hiding by a river,
Camouflaged in between the trees,
Waiting for a moving meal,
Watching and waiting
Until its dinner arrives.
A line of blood through the forest,
Leading to its once living meal.

Michael Levy (15)
Wednesfield High School

THE PARK

Sit among the trees
Watching people going by,
Kite flying so high.

Dogs chasing footballs,
Ducks swimming for their breadcrumbs,
They all pass me by.

Jennifer Franklin (15)
Wednesfield High School